Ever Between the Light and Dark

ISBN 9798742943822

Cover art by Alexander Lowe

Written and edited by Alexander Lowe

Published through Kindle Direct Publishing.

Ever Between the Light and Dark

Alexander Lowe

Kindle Direct Publishing

Contents

Chapter I: The Early Days

Chapter II: Echoes of Inspiration

Chapter III: Of Leaf and Tree

Chapter IV: Plumbing the Abyss

Chapter V: Glimpses of Hope

This page is intentionally left blank

Dedication

To Lynn Doyle, Bruce Weigl, and Joseph Bathanti: Thank you all for mentoring me in this beautiful art form.

To my parents, for continually supporting me.

To Dublin the Wheaten Terrier. You were taken too soon. If heaven is just, I'll see you there.

Chapter I: The Early Days

Preface

Aside from the odd poem I would write for an assignment in school, the first time I wrote a poem that felt like it came from the soul was during my junior year of high school. In my AP English class, we were tasked with writing a poem in any style we wanted but it needed to be about something that meant a lot to us. I decided to write about the mountains. During my freshman and sophomore years of high school, my dad and I went camping most weekends during the later spring, summer, and fall. I loved the mountains since I was a kid, but I gained a whole new appreciation for them when I decided to live in them, even if it was only for a weekend. This appreciation led me to write "The Spirit of the Mountains". I certainly don't think it is anything remarkable as a poem, but I have decided to include it to help illustrate the progression of my own writing as well as include the first step in a long affair with poetry.

I would not revisit poetry again until my junior year of college at Appalachian State University. Out of all the classes I took, none were more boring to me than British Literature. Something about the dry and stuffy nature of *The Anatomy of Melancholy* made me want to leap out of the window of the fifth floor of Sanford Hall. Instead of making that foolish decision, I decided to occupy my mind with poetry. I am not entirely sure which poem I wrote first, but I am fairly certain that it was "As the World Shakes". I wrote a series of poems all using two six-line stanzas with some sort of convoluted rhyme scheme that I thought was *genius* at the time. While these poems come off as amateurish, I still think I was able to capture truth about each poem's subject and included some images of which I am still proud.

Finally, there is a selection of poems that I do not remember ever writing. I do not know when or where in my life they were written except that it was in my formative poetry career. I am not sure as to my original meaning with several poems. For instance, "The Drop" is a poem that I have only the vaguest of recollections writing. I do know that it was the first time I played with how the poem was visually presented on the page. It was the genesis for a common technique I have found myself utilizing wherein the physical position of the words and breaks on the page are part of the story.

My first poems are undoubtedly not going to be hailed down through the ages as emblematic of a master at work. However, I believe that for a tree to grow, first a seed must be planted. I believe we must first look to the seed to understand the tree.

Spirit of the Mountains

The powdered caps of the mountains
welcome me to a peaceful place.
Their chill winds set my spirit free
as they wind their way through forest and rock.
The sound of trickling water from a quaint stream
is the soundtrack to serenity itself.
The tranquility of these mountains satisfy.
Cool, fresh air and sunflower seeds
intertwine like the sacred respect between bear and deer.
The chemistry of life congeals into synchronicity.
As the grasps of night steal the day,
cold arrives, bathed in the moon's evanescence.
From Spring to Winter the colors change,
a beautiful rainbow to remind us of the cycle of life.
The cool breeze echoes a haunting tone of times past,
with various memories, once amassed then forgotten.
When I look around the valleys, home isn't far,
up on top of the mountains, free and alone.

As the World Shakes

A suppressive haze instills
as burning ice pumps through veins.
An infinite plain, forever stretching onward,
As faces blank and stare at me—drowning me.
Fetid landslides vomit forth.
I'd rather have death win this round.

My convulsions are earthquakes,
unleashing cataclysmic tremors, white lightning.
The aftershocks are flashes, the cause of my fall,
as I gasp, every breath a battle.
My sights are like a narrowing hall.
I fall as the world shakes.

The Incredible Force of Joy

The indescribable fathoms
and a contentment unmatched,
overwhelms the senses,
renders darkness detached,
like clouds parted by
the rising sun.

The pains of a little boy,
or the tumults of despair—
sorrow or death—
could never compare
to the all enduring
incredible force of joy.

Light to the Moth

Gray wisps beckon on the end.
Droning are the pits and pats.
Despair in those summer days,
watching rain through moldy slats.
Quintessence wains, it starts to fade,
broken minds that cannot mend.

Seasons gone, Autumnal loss.
In latter days falls the sky,
Clouded pools gather around.
By sharp edge so that I may die
to lift my soul, heaven from ground,
Like light flies to mottled moth.

The Trappings of Flesh

When life chooses to reveal
the trappings of flesh—
the temple of self—
remember the blessings,
for most will fall
when trouble gapes its flapping maw.

Delusions will cloud,
that falsify life,
and eat you alive.
Strife's impediments will say:
"You must die
to truly see."

The Sun Is Almost Here

The sun is almost here.
I can see it peeking through.
The rain will leave
as the rays break the gloom.
The trees sway to each other whispering that
respite is almost here.

The vibrancy of life
always will return.
As trees grow new leaves
when the Winter leaves,
and Spring awakens,
the sun will shine again.

Unto Me, Death!

Hope ebbs
convulsions flow
terror returns
promising me no help to come.
To be slain would
gain preference to coping.

This pit of vast depths
that swallows all dreams—
dark devouring light—
echoes my screams.
The scourge of Despair's call mimics:
"Unto me, death!"

The Eye's Knit

The flesh curtain is falling
from chemically induced weight.
The time of the sheep draws nigh,
subject to the reverie's rule.
Between bliss and snapping maws,
the dawn sounds time's call.

The Old Man sits,
bringing forth the next night.
Laconic legs fail
to the sting of Weary's knife
as the pale sun
weaves the eye's knit.

Nightmare Forever

It is exploding. It's coming to a head.
The pressure is ever-building,
a liquid fire inside.
Life no longer seems willing
to hold its grip.
Rationality is eroding.

Will it ever get better?
Could it ever be the same?
Everything spirals
at tip of Life's knife.
Life is but a dream,
a nightmare forever.

Earth's Latter Theme

The cold steps through me
as the Earth sighs,
no matter the layers.
Breath from the skies,
so unmoving are its concerns,
its skin as a tree.

The cloud's dandruff,
frigid as the ninth circle,
are temptations like that of the hunger tower.
Death's looming scythe
deadens flowers and signals:
the Earth's latter theme.

Break the Fast

What contentment, feeling oneness
as the stomach is sated!
Power fluctuates,
caloric transformation to energetic pins.
Concentration now pinpointing
as dawn becomes day.

Better than the rest.
Better than rest.
A joyous time
to reflect on things
and succumb to thyme.
Time to break the fast!

The First Song

A time of temporary end
draws ever-near.
Preparation, or the lack of it
is paid off with fear or joy:
the end of a winding track
and payment for sin.

Skills will be tested,
built, and further honed.
The brain will be stretched far and long
to reflect what was gained.
The first of many swan songs signal
that life begins and time kills.

I'm Coming Home

November air flows
making me think
of my home.

Leaving before the snow
to that place.

Cozy warm drinks.
Laughter makes the air breathe.

I'm coming home

.

When lost and alone,
I want to flee,
home to them.

I want to sail there,
where I can say:
I'm home.

The Drop

the wait that comes before the drop is the longest you'll ever face.
like a roller coaster climbing a slope before sending you hurtling
down to the
ground,
each second a small eternity punctuated by pangs of excitement.
uncertainty. terror? Then when you crest the summit you

drop.

Climbing

To put words to paper
easily comes to some.
For others,
each word is an Everest to surmount,
trying to chain them together without
stumbling and falling over an Alp
or a Himalayan mound.
I must surmount every mountain;
every hill must be conquered.
The mark of a writer
is to climb
until there is nothing left to climb.

Observe and See

Beyond the sea, amongst the trees,
rivers cold, the meadows call
from earth to sky, eternity,
the mountain peaks, snowcapped and tall.

Rage

Rage is like a tornado
tearing through a home,
splitting family.
Beware the tornado.

Chapter II: Echoes of Inspiration

Preface

A writer will inevitably become a conglomeration of their influences mixed with their own unique voice. No writer has ever written a book without any influence. I find that influences do not simply just come from other writers, but from a multitude of sources. For instance, I am an avid video game player. Being able to place oneself in a narrative makes me feel immersed in a story rather than being a passive onlooker as I would with a movie. Video games, to me, are as close as I can come to reading a book as far as immersion.

All the poems in this section are directly inspired by books, video games, or a synthesis of the two. I found the *Dark Souls* series to be a particularly inspiring subject for poetry. I originally had four or five poems inspired from it, but I found many of the topics I covered in them were the same, so I took the unique parts of the poems and meshed them together to create a cohesive story.

The Lord of the Rings is a likewise interesting property to me. One of the first movies I ever remember going to the theatre to see was *The Fellowship of the Ring*. I played with *The Lord of the Rings* action figures when I was a kid. I have played just about every video game based on the series. In fact, I am a long-time player of *The Lord of the Rings Online*—an MMORPG where I have essentially lived in Middle-Earth for a disturbing portion of my life. My poems "The Shores of Evendim", "Reclaiming Home", Song of the Wayfarer", and part of "The Barrow-Wight" are fruits of my infatuation with Tolkien's world.

Two poems in this section were written for my poetry classes while earning my degree. "Misfortune, and Other Ill-Gotten Gains" is inspired by children's story "Jack and the Beanstalk". I decided to make the giant a sympathetic character and write from his perspective. "Rebuilding Babel" is a poem which *quintessentially* requires context. This poem is based on Paul Auster's *City of Glass* and was my "artistic transformation" of the book for my final project in a class simply titled

"Great Books" (plot twist: there was only a singular great book and many mediocre ones).

While the poems in this chapter are inspired by other works of art, I believe they have merit on their own meaning so don't feel intimidated if you have not acquainted yourself with the property upon which the poem is based.

Zweihander

When steel sings
and blades dance,
the game of life can begin.
I am surrounded on all sides by terrors
and the abyss grasps my feet.
The way is shut and bound by evil.
In my sword I trust—
my lifeline between life and death.
Though cruel machinations may cripple my body,
and to time my brain will succumb,
conquest will free the inner beast
and blood lust will tear through my inner peace.
Through conflict, my demons will awake.

Fires Fade Until Only Embers Remain

A new dawn's arising,
Embers fade and ashes
take to the wind.

Hollows rise,
An exodus.
Awakening the king.
We will die
just to rise again
to wipe away the sin.
Usurpation of the throne,
four strong must die to pay
the debt.

From the heights where
the dragons fly,
to the fiery depths
where the demons reign as kings,
the great valleys of ice
will not impede the usurper of the gods.

The clash of blades
sends echoes to our future.
A cycle of life and death,
an endless circle trapping us all.
The lands stay but their
names change
reminding us of those echoes.
Cinders, ashes, embers –
different names for the same thing.

The tolling of the bell announces awakening.
Halls once fair and pure will dim and die.
The world is changing, and the fires far grow dimmer by the day.
Down in the swamps, festering blight consumes our world,
gnawing life away, like life itself is consumed by time.
Cycles of change come and go, and we are helpless to stop them.
Embrace or deny, to defy or acquiesce, love or hate;
the choice must be made.
Ages of fire soon come,
casting the world in shadows, distorting
concrete obsessions into dancing mirages,
Plato's cave becoming reality.
Perhaps the age of man,
of darkness,
must come for life to truly flourish.
Would it be better to be blind in the dark or be fooled by the light?
The choice will fall to the chosen
because the fires are fading.
To hold high the flame
or beckon the dark?

The Shores of Evendim

As a blue-tinged tongue licks the banks,
the salty, storied past is revealed.
The spires of Annúminas protrude up—
once a great city, now like a dead spider's legs flung upward,
rotting and perfuming the air with their rancidity.
From the island of Tinnudir, hope rises with the tides.
The thought of reclaiming the kingdom softens brittle bones
and applies poultices to ancestor's memories—
passed down in the ever-fading reminders
on the walls of ruins and minds.
Just as the dwarves from ages past seek to reclaim their forgotten halls,
men, too, strive forward through the tumults and waves
to reach the farthest shores of Evendim
and take their homes back again.

The crystal waters tell stories of strife,
pockmarked by interloping masts.
She too once dwelled here, that Lady of the Lake.
Only the waterfalls sing her praises now,
the splashes of water on rock beating out the chant of nature.
Further on the western shore,
far above Emyn Uial's door,
the giants sing and slowly stoop,
waiting for their master's call—
a wild call. A call from the roots of the earth,
deeper than the earth itself.
Their homes are overgrown,
entangled with cruelty, huorns and beasts,
but Northern hatred is what binds the evil to their frames.
The song of a fallen kingdom rings through the depths.
The ripples on the lake are reminders of what has been lost.
Tyl Annûn will be our sanctum again,
when Angmar is returned to the state before life,
and we are prepared on this day to die.

The Barrow-Wight

We all fear the barrow-wight
creeping through the upstairs halls.
Before our bath, we hear a creak,
and seek refuge from the rancor call.
I know he lurks just up ahead—
the living soul of some undead—
around the corner, so we peek to see what evil foot befalls.
There he is with rag in hand—
damp, its thrown, where will it land?
On me! I'm trapped under his spell.
Off to lands where undead dwell.
Should I wake before I die,
in a land I'll be where shadows lie.
Crept upon by mottled cloth,
no emancipation through the moth.
Among these ruins shall I lay,
to hunt and haunt those that sleep.
When night comes, supplanting day,
From down and barrow, I will leap.

Reclaiming Home

What does it mean to be home?

Home is where family is,
where happiness is abundant,
and love saturates the air,
like cinnamon and clove on an autumn day.

Home is where our values and thoughts
are exchanged and honed.
Where opinions can be shared with dinner rolls,
and there are always second helpings of discussion.

Home is where sleep can be found without fear.
The darkness takes no hold in a home.
The creatures that grip us in the night can't
grasp our elusive contentment and twist it.

Where is our home?
Our home is where love is cold,
where the food is rotten,
where darkness reigns king.

Our home is lost.
Our home was taken.
Our home is not home.

Song of the Wayfarer

I've seen marshes.
Miserable.
Sneaky.
Always looking to add you
to their collection of muck-covered secrets,
long lost and buried under scum.

I've seen mountains.
Lonely.
Isolated.
Instilling a sense of freedom,
but one wrong move
and you'll find yourself falling.

I've seen the plains.
Freedom.
Liberating.
A canvas for expression and creativity
stretching infinitely beyond the edge of sight,
the unknown swallowing unbridled passion.

I've seen the forests.
Confusion.
Beauty.
The green umbrellas form a thick layer,
sheltering us from storms, but also leading astray
wanderers because of their conformity.

I've seen the sea.
Longing.
Awaiting.
Beautiful, like nightshade, and terrifying just the same,
wonders both sinister and pure coexist,
an aquatic neural net.

I've seen the world.
I've traveled every road.
All paths are beset by evil
and all shortcuts are best left undisturbed.
The long road continues on,
toward the infinite horizon.

Rebuilding Babel

I'll always wonder where he went,
that empty plot where he laid
for days
giving shape to what had become of him.
I wonder…
did he know it? His madness, I mean.
Or maybe we're the mad ones.
Perhaps his double vision
truly framed things quintessentially:
the cracked concrete slabs,
the mindless day-walking fools,
caught up in their own affairs
not noticing the unsightly monolith—
a confusing collection of stone and syllables—
constructed around their own feet
like briars creeping up the sides of a plant,
choking out life,
subjugating the harvest,
betraying it to pestilence and plague.
Yes.
I think perhaps he was the only one among us,
the only one who really understood what was happening.
He saw the connections,
the doublings,
the faults in the foundations,
slowly eroding.
All artists are tormented, sure,
so, I believe he was no different.
He was both Cain and Adam,
a murderer and a victim to his own actions.
Except when Abel was killed, Adam then lost himself.
No longer was he Adam, but Daniel Quinn.
No longer was he Cain, but Max Work.
No longer was he Man, but Babel.

His loss was like God's confoundment of man.
Quinn no longer spoke one language, but thousands.
He was Jew and he was Greek.
He was human and he was animal.
He was a writer and he was written.
For he, too, only remains in a scrawl
across a few hundred pages
of a crumpled red notebook.
I'll always wonder where he went.
I still wonder where he might be going.

Misfortune, and Other Ill-Gotten Gains

Sometimes a man just wants to be left alone
to dream of riches of heaven and earth.
The common man is allowed to follow his dreams,
while afflicted giants like me
must suffer. All that was once
is now never, elusive as wind, an ether, palpable
but never containable. Misfortune seems to show
itself on the rolling tides of change. Ever since the beanstalk—
that blot of inconformity—has made its presence known,
I've been drowning in the tide as my fortunes wane
with the moon. First it was my gold, fairly won
in a game of chance. Second it was my magic hen,
a gift of God, blessing the heavenly treasures
from within, virtue embodied. Only my harp remains.
This time misfortune shall not have its way.
This time, a penance will be paid for another's gain
and this giant will have his day.

In the Shadow of Fear

In that place where the bridge overhead casts a shadow
down upon our simple home,
echoes scream across dimensions.
The world is strange.
Blight and plague eat away at afflicted
and un-afflicted just the same.
Beings beyond sight and mind interlope,
edging into the vestiges of our world.
Day and night, we watch as screams,
otherworldly, incomprehensible,
wrench themselves from an incompatible host,
clawing free out of the castle windows
and taking root at our doors, waiting,
poised with a knife, ready to strike
when we poke our heads out to see.
I fear we've been abandoned, left to suffer for some unknown crime.
I can hear the chantry bells. They call us, knowing we must come.
Their toll sounds all too familiar. Perhaps they wield knives too.

White, Silver, Red

Can two unlike subjects understand one another?
I can no more be you than a rock a tree.

Where I go, blood rains and screams follow.
Where you go, laughter erupts, and the sun comes out.

I am the white wolf and you are the loving farm dog,
Racing out to greet its owners while I eat the sheep.

You wield one sword, I wield two—one for you,
And one for those toward whom your sword will fail.

Your poison is my steroid, afflictions removed,
Constitution strengthened; senses opened up.

You spit on me, but when the moon waxes full,
And the horrors creep out, you call out in help.

I've walked all life's roads and seen those around me die.
That is my job, my life's journey, my destiny.

The Sight of Sound

The gravitational field is not diffused through space;
The gravitational field is space itself.
Time and dimensions flood effervescently through cosmic space,
Shining, visible and tangible.
What does light feel like?
It feels like color. It feels like sensation.
Lasting visages of an instant of supernova light remains,
Sensing our sensations.
Feeling our feelings.
A true hallucination speaks softly and slowly,
It is in the spaces and between them.
It isn't drug through the space,
It is the space.
Selah.

Chapter III: Of Leaf and Tree

Preface

When I first began writing about nature, I felt like I finally found my voice as a writer. I'm not so sure a writer ever finds their voice now. I view it as an ever-evolving presence. I am part of the last generation that grew up without a cellphone as an ever-present companion. One benefit of this was that I played outside a lot as a kid. When our church let out on Saturday (I went to an Adventist church for the first decade or so of my life), my family would frequently drive up to the mountains. Sometimes we would simply walk around the Bass Lake near Moses Cone National Park. Sometimes I would live out my fantasy of being a cowboy at Tweetsie Railroad. All trips would end at Greene's Trading Post with boiled peanuts. These trips engendered a love for nature within me.

I find nature is a perfect vehicle for allegory, imagery, symbolism, and whatever other stuffy terms one wants to apply to poetry to over-analyze it. I have found that for everything in my life, there has been a perfect analog for it in nature.

Nature, at least from my beliefs and my own understanding of the world, is ambivalent. Nothing within nature seems to have inherently evil intent or good intent. It is really a matter of perspective on how to interpret how it affects the world. With that in mind, the following poems show both light and darkness through the lens of ambivalence. Few things are wholly evil, and few things are wholly good. It is only through neutrality that we can discover the true intentions (or at least our best guess as to them) of something.

The Saga of the Seasons

Awakening

It is with meekness that the buds
inch forth their heads from the womb
of Mother earth, breathing in
the nectar of the wind for the first time.

A flower and tree share habitation,
their roots crossing, tickling each other.
Both benefit from nutrients left
by forbearers, both native and interloper.

As animals create offspring,
so too does greenery follow suit.
They come together, sending forth jubilation,
accelerating to pinnacle before returning to familiar frontiers.

Persistence

Most have awakened and drunk the nectar
that both Mother Earth and Father Sun gifted.
Father swells in pride, beaming onto the face
of his children and wife, nourishing further.

But Father knows little of what his mirth furthers.
The warmth he provides for growth, stifles.
The energy he supplies for life, exhausts.
He doesn't know his love kills his family.

But onward he shines, and his children are grateful,
for if his shine were to ebb, the bite of night would arrive,
overgrowth would choke, thorns pierce,
and nightshade and nightingale would be the only dwellers.

Metamorphosis

Life has had its stay.
The year descends toward diminuendo.
Vibrant greens blush to crimson,
cadmium, ochre, and violet.

Brown hair and fur has waxed white like moonlight,
now waning as less returns each season.
Mother Earth lets out a sigh as she collapses
under the weight of her own children.

Mother is tired and drained, only dregs left
of her once opulent splendor reflecting in the elms,
the winds, shadows, and waters.
She must leave them and rest.

Homesick

Where have Mother and Father gone?
It seemed just a moment since they embraced us.
Now it is a cold world. My brothers and sisters die.
We weren't ready to be on our own.

Our forest choir fades to whispers,
and whispers turn to wind.
The only voices singing
are our howls of grief.

As Mother and Father return from slumber,
they find a graveyard filled with children.
Bark and flesh alike populate graves.
Guilt.

Shall we try again? asked Mother.
But the result will remain the same replied Father. *It is insanity.*
Yes replied Mother, *but what else is there to do?*
We're all bound to it.

The Fires of Life

From the smallest sparks,
a wildfire can spring,
consuming every ounce
of fuel in its path.
My fire burns hot,
a beacon in the fray
of the ever-shifting proving grounds of life.
Once the fire gets going,
nothing can stop its advance,
except for time's exacting toll,
collected when only embers remain.
Suddenly, my tinder smolders,
it's already over,
the call having just reached my doorstep,
a knock and a scratch.
This life's journey is long,
and its path is unpredictable,
just as the flames that twist around
the ever-immolating effigy that I call Me.
This fantastic journey is worth the dreaded destination—
life's cost of admission—ultimately ending in elegy.
Life is fragile, like cinders in the wind:
glinting eyes that paint the canvas of the night sky—
the only infinite thing I see.

An Autumnal Reverie

Why is it,
when tides of change come
and arboreal hues bleed and burn,
that minds
return to times
where songs were sweeter
and our lenses of life
made all things shimmer
in the tint of the sun's light?

Perhaps browning leaves
call to our temporary nature,
as our bodies fall to dust,
fertilizing leaves that, in turn,
fall to this Great Coffin's floor,
trodden to pulp
until the noose of winter
cinches,
draining the last life from the leaves.

Gilded reveries float in the mind's stream.
Summers past are perfect constructs,
with temperatures rich and the earth's breath
strong enough for sweat to dry.
The lemonade was tart and sweet,
the skies, abstract with beauty,
the bugs let us be, watching from afar,
and things were slower with the whole world ahead,
where the only worries of tomorrow
faded into worries of the past.
Lethargy was just an opportunity
for a warm drink, soft chair, and good book
on a cozy night.

The trees are bare now—
relinquishing their weight
to perceived time—
that ever-closer-creeping death knell.
To a lonely plot I plod, pondering the passage
of this fleeting force
called time.
Soon to lay to rest,
I declare that
memories are lies; the past is tainted,
misconstrued to profanity.
We pass with a breath
that takes to wind and rends leaf from branch.

Now as autumnal chords play their dirge,
the winds of fall sweep through the trees,
and I tread a path into the wild,
knowing that summer was far too hot,
the chair splintered and broken,
the book boring and long,
the bugs stinging hornets,
the drink bitter poison,
and these primal pictures of lucid dreams
are crudely scrawled on the tombstone of my mind.

What Luna Sees, What Sol Ignores

I see her watching
when she knows she isn't
supposed to,
peeking through the blinds of day
to see what all the fuss is about,
and why *he* gets all the credit.
She looks at the mountains.
Putrid asphalt rivulets leak from the corners
of a steel beast's gaping mouth
and crawl like an oozing lake of vomit
wretched forth because of Socrates' Poison.
She looks at the forests.
A circle of friends stand,
their many arms thrust out
to greet each other in embrace.
Suddenly
          one
                begins
                      to
                         tip
                            over until he lies horizontal on his mother.
In his Mother's arms, she inaudibly screams
through browning leaves and heated winds.
She looks at the seas
but quickly averts her eyes.
Those pelagic depths,
defiled as Philomel,
their tongues torn terribly, and flowers ripped by tombèd bipeds.
She saw these things and despaired.

> *Woe be the tides of Sol*
> *whose light doth illuminate*
> *our excoriated and razed*
> *children and grandchildren.*
> *Damn thee Sol!*

Thou art the spec in
my eye!
If only Lethe could rip away
the ignorance
of your self-blinded eyes
that I may lay down and die.
You wretched ignorant eye.
She bowed her head from Sol's light,
disappearing from my sight.
Did her eyes she pluck
so that through even her dim gaze
naught could be seen
and the night be none the wiser to the day's offenses?

Clearing Muck from the Bottom of a Pond

I cleared the muck away
from the bottom of the pond
on a warm summer's day,
to wash the filth away.
I'd make a difference this way,
scooping the algae of the pond
to clear the filth away
from the bottom. Of the pond,

I can say precious little
because there is little to be said
of ponds, save for their bottom's spittle,
green and lumpy, with beauty little,
and ponderous riddle
and the dead, of which can be said
naught but a little;
their actions are what is said.

The living's words are real,
but the dead have no words
and only deeds remain unveiled;
only the actions are real.
The dead brokered the deal
which couldn't have been with words,
imaginary, unreal.
Future death sounds in the words.

I cleared the muck away
from the bottom of the pond
on a warm summer's day
to chase fear away
that some soon day,
from the bottom of the pond,
I would be scraped away,
a stain on the bottom of a pond.

The Twilight Hours

During those precious few hours,
those before the rising of the sun
or the triumph of day over night,
all is gray.
Barely visible, all colors seem
to bleed away, leaving a shell
in their place.
It is during this time,
when no other living creature stirs,
that I see the true color of life.

I drift,
sailing at sea on distant currents,
listening to the shifting waves beneath,
their lapping and plopping.
The pitch bruises of the night
fade,
replaced by the crimson cheeks of dawn,
slowly pushing the moon under the water,
back into its kingdom of black.
Pelagic tar becomes living water,
stirring life, propelling it to glorification.
With the dawn I know the tides.
I know from whence I came
and to what port I travel.
My eyes burn with tiredness,
amplified by the mirror ocean.
I think I might like to sleep a while,
rocked gently, back and forth,
like a mother rocking her baby—
like God protecting Noah.
I will wake up at my home,
free of worry,
ready to continue my work.

I Can Move Mountains

The power is in me
to heave the earth from the soil
and send it resting
in the domain of the clouds.
We are our own gods
in the works we create.
God made the mountains
through tectonic inception,
and I make them
through electronic transmission.
We form the creation from within us
sending it to rest upon the page
while we remain spent
from the toil.
God is perfect
but I am flawed
and so is my creation.
I strive and work to ascend the peak
only to roll down, a bigger mess each time,
and find my work in ruins,
tatters of my own mind rent to puddles.
each time, I know a little better.
I can avoid the loose rocks
and sheer cliffs on my ascent to the summit.
I can't reach the top,
so I must choose to continue to go on,
or give up and let the mountain conquer me.

The Mouse

I often wonder why God created mice.
They don't really seem to serve a function
aside from absconding with a petrified chip,
fallen and forgotten beneath a garbage can at the park.
How can such a small creature be of any significance?

Animals get even less significant than mice too.
I'll applaud if you can give me one
good reason that gnats exist.
They're always getting in the coffee,
left in the pot after breakfast.

An even more baffling creature is the stink bug.
I'd be hard-pressed to find any use for those.
Even an internet search reveals that their only
natural predator is a wasp—
yet another useless creature.

But I have a hunch as to why these things exist.
Just as we are creative, God is too.
When the world was chiseled and painted,
God didn't want it to get boring
so He gave us a multitude to see.

Like the mouse.

Big as an Acorn, Small as a Tree

We all grow up reaching toward the sun
hoping that someday we will reach the top.
Extended limbs and weathered trunks alike,
reach upward to grasp the great divine.
Impending frost leaves us shivering
as we shrink, forever writhing alone.
Other's roots are ripped out,
the rot taking its final toll.
We never will capture the sun's essence,
though never will we cease to take a stand
and stretch beyond capacity's limit.
The sun warms best when you come near its shine,
so imbibe in its divine glow:
bask in its eternal rays of light.

Shortcut

Slowly I traveled
through a snow tinted valley—
each step, another victory.
A shortcut, a fold in the map,
a wormhole to the other side—
yet, a piece of my humanity was lost for it.
The darkness had weight to it,
like the pressure that builds up in one's ears
when diving deep into the sea,
lost in wonder at the fathomless depths
and unequaled beauty of the pelagic concert
of marine life.
At first, the shortcut seems worth it.
The water is clear, or the path slopes down.
The waves are calm, or the thicket thins.
Then, like a rabbit who sees the shadow of a hawk,
too late,
you see the shadow of something sinister.
Like a shark.
Or a bear.
The shortcut is always beset by dangers.
They equal or outweigh the prize.
Perhaps it would have been best
to take the long way around.

Zebra at the Genesis

All was still.
All was calm.
The faces of the waters stood silent,
like mirrors, reflecting the expanse
He called the sky and the light
He called day.
Trees stood waiting,
their newly formed bodies eagerly curious to see what would happen
next.
The unnamed beast
with black and white stripes
pensively, its eyes cautious, judges the dust man.

To the Specs Below

A small romance of clouds
In empty skies
For strange aeons may come
Which eternal lie.

And I wondered…

As lonely as a cloud
may be,
we still converge and sing wet songs.
The heat makes us fluff up,
puffing out, declaring our might.
The cold makes us small
and bitter,
spitting forth our protests in slick frozen pools.
When the skies split, our anger jolts out,
bolting into the upright things below.
They after all, are just the things below,
not of us clouds
prostrate in the ether.

Nature Walk

through fields of gold and forgotten
memories she walked her mind as a stream
nearby a babbling brook lolled its lazy tongue
what could the clouds mean
any number of gods could be calling
as the last fingers of sunset lost their grip
on the edge of the horizon
she knew which God had sent the message

The Last Snow

There it came,
twirling and dancing its way,
down from the sky to
its resting place on the boy's cold nose
There it sat
and then it melted—
its life like the length of a
match burning.
Though only living a second, it
danced with the vigor
that only a snowflake could.

The Trail

I walked the trail,
shielded by trees,
onward to the meadow.
That path was obscured,
blanketed in pine needles,
and the birds sang their song
while I walked the trail for
the last time.

Roots

When the wind comes,
those without roots will be blown away.
When the floods come,
those who don't stand tall will drown.
When the blizzards come,
those without depth will freeze.
In all facets, be prepared
or be destroyed by adversity.

Chapter IV: Plumbing the Abyss

Preface

"Why don't you write something positive?" is a phrase with which I am sure many writers of poetry are familiar. I always respond by saying, "Where is the fun in a movie without conflict?" Many of my poems come from darkness, both figuratively and literally. My junior year of college was when I found out that I had depression. After accidentally running over my dog in my car, I discovered a well a darkness so deep that it felt like I would never crawl out. It would not go away, even after my grieving went away. It was specter that used me as a puppet. Eventually, I got on medication and it has helped immensely. I should probably also be in therapy.

In addition to my clinical darkness, I also fluctuate between an optimistic pessimist and a pessimistic optimist. I've worked on my disposition and have got it to a point where I feel happy nearly every day and don't view life as completely suffering, but the dourness is still within me.

Of course, it also does not help that the media that I like best focuses on the dark and macabre. I love horror movies and horror video games. Visually, I like morbid art. *Saturn Devouring His Son* is one of my favorite paintings. Halloween is my favorite holiday. I listen to death metal, horrorcore, and lots of grim music.

All these factors coalesce into the poems in the next section. While I believe that we should aspire to the light, we should also learn from the darkness to know what to avoid and how to deal with those who do not aspire to the light.

Winning the Lottery

A lottery drawing was held on December 1, 1969, at Selective Service National Headquarters in Washington, D.C. This event determined the order of call for induction during calendar year 1970; that is, for registrants born between January 1, 1944, and December 31, 1950. There were 366 blue plastic capsules containing birth dates placed in a large glass container and drawn by hand to assign order-of-call numbers to all men within the 18-26 age range specified in Selective Service law.
-The Selective Service

I saw Professor Weider in the grocery store.
It's always odd to see someone
in a place you don't expect them.
Turning an aisle, I stood at the junction
between rice and pasta,
trying to recall whether I had the ziti
in the little blue box on my shelf.
Then I spotted him.
His salt and pepper hair
cascaded down to his shoulders
and his jazz hands tapped
tapped, tapped
a rhythm to set a pace to his walk.
When he saw me, the wrinkles
around his mouth—
distinguished folds that parted
when he smiled—scrunched.
It was that same smile he gave me last month
when he told me that he didn't want to
talk about that time during the war
after he had been ripped from his family
when he heard his birthday on the radio in 1970,
unlucky enough to be born on July 9,
one of the first of 1,766,910 lucky winners
to be shipped off to war,
where his best friend got syphilis

from a prostitute
sent by the Viet Cong,
resulting in his death
after the penicillin failed;
where he saw his commanding officer
step on a toe-popper
that turned his foot from fortress to tatters,
and nicked his femoral artery,
leaving him to bleed out
twenty minutes away from medical.
Hey Professor, I said,
tension feeling like squirming squids in my stomach.
Hello he chimed. *Getting groceries?*
Yep, I replied, hoping he would just go.
I'll see you in class Monday, I said, and hustled away.
I've seen him in other places,
on other faces.
I've seen him on the blank stare of my uncle.
I've seen him on the clerk scanning my groceries.
Your total is $7.07.
7/07.
If only he'd been born two days earlier.

History Is Written in Pencil

How do I know what to believe
when history written in pencil
can be erased and replaced?
Truth depends on the author.

When history is written in pencil
fact can be scrawled out and revised.
Truth depends on the author,
and our pasts can be altered to lie.

Fact can be scrawled out and revised
so I write my history in pen.
My past can't be altered to lie,
by a historian deciding who wins.

I write my history in pen
so I can never revise it.
Letting a historian decide the victor
is like quartering and drawing a man.

I must never revise
history that's written in pencil.
Drawing a man and quartering his deeds
veils him in untruth.

History that's written in pencil
is all around.
Veiled untruths pass as fact,
like winning the Vietnam war

or how Christopher Columbus was a good man.
It's all around,
these fibs and half-truths,
like winning the Vietnam war.

It's all around us,
erased and replaced.
Like "winning" the Vietnam war,
how do I know who is the winner?

The Self-Destructing Self

I trace my knuckles
choosing the best
when I come to *that* question on an exam,
a surprise examination of knowledge.
I know the satisfaction
comes from errors in my brain's software.
I rock the knuckle
till my fingers numb
and knuckles blush.

I sink my teeth
into my bottom lip,
when I revise a poem,
not knowing what to write next.
I repeat time and again,
knowing the satisfaction
sparks from a loose wire in my circuitry.
I chew until my lips blister
and pain ceases my prostration.

I wrinkle the skin between my fingers
letting the webbing stretch, cross,
and retract
when I prepare to interact with people.
I know the satisfaction
ekes from a rusted cog in my machine
That isn't up to standard with the others
I cross until I callous,
unable to bear the feeling of my own hands.

I scrunch my top lip
to peak then valley,
feeling the whiskers scrape,
tickling my lip
when I hear screams from upstairs,
knowing it is all my fault,
knowing the satisfaction I get
from these habits come from
a complete hardware failure.

Meeting a Stranger on the Road at Night

The hour grows long,
my coffee short
as headlights carve
a window into the black
road, revealing yet another
lonely mile.
I am lost,
though many times
have I travelled this road.
My destination is sure
to be just around the next turn.
I feel like Dante,
vexed in a forest dark
and heart assailed by terrors.
If only some Virgil,
some gas station,
would guide me to paths familiar.
Instead, I am greeted by light
of another traveler.
I stare at him as our cars slow.
I believe we both know this encounter
is of some importance.
In this interlude of a moment,
his eyes survey me and I him.
Is that sorrow in his eyes,
or mere reflection?
Have our paths intertwined by fated chance
or did he know I would be here?
The trembling in my hands
rises to an earthquake
and the pit of my stomach erodes.
His path holds power—
I feel it roiling from his soft grin.
The stillness of the night is punctuated

by a horn from behind,
urging me to depart.
From the look on his face,
I believe he pitied me,
for he knew I would go,
that I would remain lost.
For he had traveled my road,
and I his,
there being only one spanning this wood.
His road will be long and treacherous.
I knew, for I have traveled it many times
in the dark.
And the pity on his face told
that he knew my road
was short
and straight
but led
to a dead
end.
His road led to paradise.
I would go into the inferno.

How Deep We Dive

It was during the spring of 2016 when I first began the longing, that desperate yearning, for the touch of the sea. I parted the water and ventured to *that place*—the place where we all must venture when time strikes our fancy; the place where the water runs deepest. I don't remember when I dove in, if in fact that was how my flesh met the glassy surface of the ocean. Perhaps I slipped on the dregs of my own mind. Perhaps I was seized and cast into the depths. It always starts off calmly as the water filters through you, pores opened to wind tunnels to let in the salt. The ocean's caress is soft and lulling, a siren's song to lure the soul to sleep so that leviathans may emerge, unseen. Then, when the clarity of the sea seems at its clearest, the tempest strikes, the mirror breaks, and what was once thought clear becomes opaque. In one such time, I am slammed to the depths, a tidal transformation. The pressure seizes me, blowing my insides out into the water. Sharks begin to swarm, smelling my blood, my fear, my vulnerability, and things unseen reach up to waylay me. My legs become entangled—no, they become the tangled mass of kelp groping up from the floor. I'm taken lower and lower. Water flows through me and my lungs. The pressure turns my mind into a parasite that begins to devour my own body from within. Every time I expect something different. I don't know how I'll return. I have to hope that once the sea has devoured me, there will be something left to float to the surface.

The Death of Dublin the Wheaten Terrier: An Elegy

Through fields of wheat you ran,
past the barn and through the dell,
floppy ears tracing the air.
Day and night you dreamt of me,
twitching your nose, too large for your head,
awaiting my return home.
You were ready to pounce,
oversized paws poised to pin me down
and lavish me with your welcomed kisses.
Whether snow or shower, you took life
and turned its frown to a smile.
Your life flashed and faded,
gone without warning,
robbed before realized.
Our shared memories will reverberate,
echoes upon the empty chamber of my mind.
My pain and sorrow will subside,
but your puzzle piece will always
be missing from my heart.

Carry on through pastures
with fleet paws that usher you onward
beyond this worldly mirror,
Over bridges and little rivers
babbling and crying.
You accepted me the way I was
and carried my worries in your eyes.
Now you're gone and the spaces in the house
are missing their light.
The air is stale, my voice flat,
without you to illuminate it
with a smile of two sharp canine teeth
and a long lazy tongue to bridge the gap between them.

Your kind gaze was always soothing,
expressing your sentiments in ways that words can't.
Your eyes were two jewels of hot chocolate
that begged for pancakes.
To run my fingers through your golden hair,
savoring the texture, as soft as the morning's light,
was to dwell in comfort itself.
Your growls and bugles,
taken for granted at their utterance,
are now remembered as symphonies.
The last embrace we shared,
I carry to eternity,
for when I am as you are now,
I will carry you always.

In a Mirror Dimly

Upon an abyss I came,
a yawn of darkness threating to swallow all
who passed through it.
Upon the edge of this ravine I stood.

It whispers soft and serene,
coaxing me to embrace its caress.
I see scaffolds,
ruins built upon desolation.
Who built them?
What could possess us children of light
to dwell within shadow?
I look down in the ravine and made out horrors—
horrid creatures, revolting to every sense.

Yet…

to me they seem acquainted,
to me they beckon,
as if welcoming me home.
I dangle a foot over the ledge, contemplating.
Suddenly, I feel a hand upon my shoulder.
Tis a stranger.
He smiles at me, pointing at
          the abyss.
"Have you been there?" He plies.
"No," I reply.
"Where are you now?" He asks. "Look up."
I gaze up to see myself looking down at me
in disgust.
"You are here, and lost your way it seems,"
the stranger says.
"You once knew these ruins as home,
but you left once,
twice,

many times,
until you were as Dante,
midway upon the journey of our life,
within a forest dark,
with the straightforward path lost
and a foot held in hell.
Lucky for you, I know a way out,
and if you follow me,
I built a bridge to cross the abyss."
He holds His hand out to me.
"Come."

The Obsidian Homunculus

I traverse the wastes
seeking solace from imminence.
This rocky terrace provides no cover,
leaving me exposed to the sun's radiation.
Darkness will soon shroud
and the funeral of night will proceed.
Its congregation of wispy black
carries pitch eyes and glinting maws,
the breath of tombs and saliva wafting, breaching.
I must make myself wind,
unseen but present,
deadly but concealed,
blatant but natural.
I carry on.

Approaching a canyon,
I see it:
monolith;
deity;
incongruous angles converging,
forming fissures of void.
It is abhorrent,
its black armor gleaming
as spires erupt out,
jagged, crooked,
not wholly identifiable.
The stench of sulfur, acrid and burning,
sets my nostrils aflame.

The thing stands betwixt the canyon's crack,
barring entrance and escape, unmoving, staunch—
rancorous.
Just considering the pits of its eyes—
like rotten apples cores left to rot in the heat—

leaves me acknowledging all things:
the grease from my oil duster—
the odor of my unwashed flesh—
putrid pools of radiated water—
a beast's decaying corpse.
A cosmic truth unravels
Laying bare the rotten veil
behind the black heart of the universe
as it pulses and beats its rotten din.
As night crawls up from the horizon,
drowning out the sun,
the monstrosity shifts,
and I remember why we fear the dark.

Yellow House

That old yellowed house down the street,
the one we ran away from
after the old creaky board on the rotting front porch squeaked
unexpectedly when we went to see if anyone lived there,
has been there ever since I was a boy, so many years ago.
Momma told me it had been there long past when she was a girl.
You know those old homes:
The ones with that odd broken window,
probably bashed in by a baseball or rock,
but you always thought that maybe some old man,
One with a drooping face and stale tobacco breath,
had broken in and was just waiting
to unload a load of buckshot into your chest.
The ones with the peeling paint
and crooked mailbox,
bent by a driver who never stopped
because poor people can't afford to sue.
The ones that always have drawn moth-eaten curtains
and some unappealing paint job
that needed a fresh coat twenty years ago.
The houses that change the neighborhood from
"That quaint little cul-de-sac" to
"That one with the serial killer house."
I've often thought about who might have lived in that house.
Did anyone even live in it at all?
I wonder.
Maybe I'll go give it a tap on the door one of these days.

A Letter from a Friend

I was there when you were born,
but you did not know of me.
You sat cooing and smiling
at your mother's face.

I was there on your first day of school,
but you did not know me yet.
My friend you knew, but not I
as you saw your father pull away.

I was there when you graduated high school.
We had met a few times by then
on gray days shaded by clouds
and abstracted by time.

I was there when your dog died.
I talked to you
          and   listened,
you insisting it was your fault.

I was there when you tried to get rid of me,
when you forgot all, we had been through.
You got addicted to those pills saying:
"Depart from me, I never knew thee."

I was there when you tried to come back to me.
You said you were clean,
you went cold turkey,
but it was too much for you.

I will be there when you reach middle-age.
You will see me in the corner,
but you act like I am a specter
and tell me I am not real.

I will be there when you die.
You will be lost in your mind,
a drumbeat turning to a flat line,
and my hand will rest on your shoulder.

I have always been there.
I am with you now.
I will always be with you.
See you soon.

Your friend,
Depression

The Inner Screaming Sanctum

What would it feel like
to never be able to smile—to never see the sun,
or show pleasure, only a façade,
a parody of real joy,
when your insides scream with desire for the world to just
see you beam?
I know this world all too well.
Though I see the sun, my smiles are fleeting.

I reach out,
like a war amputee
in search of a lost limb
but phantom pains are the only response,
the body betraying
instinct.

That one day, the tolling of the bell: picture day,
I am a condemned man before a firing squad,
taking my seat on the stool.
The gun fires.

Snap.

Blind, a disappointed snap as the impact
residue spills out onto a screen—
a face captured in that split second, familiar, but not aligning
with the inner sanctum of my body.

Onlookers gather to silently judge—
piercing eyes wondering why
you're so miserable.
Why don't you smile?

Gone, but Not Forgotten

You are gone.
Gone but not forgotten.

As the spring rolled by and turned into fall,
You were there, supporting me.
As the leaves died and turned to ice,
The sky whitened and the air turned cold.

A mistake.
A mistake.
You are gone.
Gone but not forgotten.

As the New Year rolled around,
And the skies became light once more,
You were there, supporting me.
Then you were gone, like breath to wind.

You are gone.
You are gone.
You are gone but not forgotten.

Seeing death as the end of a life
is like seeing the horizon as the end of the ocean.
To continue our memory
in the hearts of those we leave behind is not to die,
but to echo throughout eternity.

Message to a Facebook User

You've a need for validation
from all across the nation.
Your posts spread like a sensation across the land,
all from the palm of your hand.
It's like a balm; it soothes your inadequacy
from some trauma inflicted by daddy or momma.
Now you paint it over.
It's a tainted cover that makes those who love you suffer.
You forsake your own brother for the appeasement of others.
Our admiration surrounds you.
What astounds me, too, is the contempt that shows through.
There's no redemption, no
way to take that hatred and turn it sacred
and make you see the gifts that abound around you.
Our praises seem seamless;
they fall flat and meaningless.
It may be mean to think this,
but I don't even know if Jesus could
remove the sullen lines etched from endless lies
that tell you that you're worthless.
You're not.
You are worthy.
We love you and want to pick you up,
stick you straight from hate to heaven,
from zero to eleven,
from stranger to brethren.
But first we need you
to acknowledge the affliction,
this addiction that enslaves you.
We can pull and tear all we like,
but we can't turn that pain to light
until you realize you're in chains.

The Sun Was in My Eyes

when the world began to shake. Between monuments of stone and trees I stood. And faded were the names on the heads, time etching away what little was left of what already fell to time. I heard a song—a dirge—a wail—as a mournful congregation passed by. They turned their heads, each staring then proceeding. I thrust my hands into the mud, slicked smooth with rain. Blood began to fall from my eyes. I wriggled my fingers, feeling the filth, ignoring my brain's clean desires. I ate the mud, feeling its grit between my teeth and on the roof of my mouth. And I screamed, but what for? For I'd end here too, under this mud, my name fading on a stone and my flesh rotting, congealing, and undergoing putrefaction, liquefying into a slurry, drunk by earth. My hands bled, nails coming free from their beds. I beat my face smearing blood, mud, and nails across my face. I vomit. I feel my stomach churn and twist, flipping as I regurgitate for the earth, feeding my worms into a pool of mud and vomit. I cry. I can't stop it. It's coming. Time is short—running out. Where are you going? Come back! I wasn't ready, wasn't finished. I had stuff to do, things to see, and people to love, know, marry, die with. No. It can't be here yet. I can't go. Life is forever. I'm invincible. I don't die. No. My hands have eyes so I can see through the mud, beyond the veil. It's not over. It all will end eventually.

My Upper Lip

It sits there
like a dead bird in winter
frozen stiff and rigid
its muscles hardened to movelessness.

When I look into a mirror
I see my face
the face that feels things
the face that experiences the joys,
the wonders, the struggles, and sweet little moments
that life has to offer.
But the face doesn't express these feelings.
Can't express these feelings.

I walk past a row of family pictures
during a return home.
I look at the faces of each loved one.
They're beaming wide with love
in the revelry of family joy.
But then I see one face.
A face
that smudges the otherwise
perfect painting that is the smiling family.
That face is pulled into something
that isn't me—
not my feelings.
My feelings are a smile.
This punk smirks
for that is all he can do.

"You have a beautiful smile," says the biased mother.
"Yeah" I say, taking the complement
with as much attention as we give an ant.

I'll never get to do that,
smile that is,
not here, anyway.
Maybe when the time is right
and the clouds give way to the infinite beyond,
I'll finally let my smile shine.
I don't know if I can,
but I'd like to.

There Are No Stars Here

I love the feel of the sand
as it is sucked from under my feet
when the water retracts back to the sea.
The solid ground becomes slurred
as the frothy surf washes over me.
The ground seems to move
with me as a passenger,
pulling me out to the depths
while all I love remains distant.

It is dark out here.
The black currents rip me
from one abyss to the next.
The beach is no longer here.
I exist among the pelagic silence.
This annexed space is different.
It makes *me* different—
a stranger to all I have met.
People stare,
noting something different,
the stagnant ocean they dwell in
now teeming with life.
There are no stars here.
Whence does the light stem?
Perhaps it is me.
Perhaps what illuminates the dark waters
comes from within my spirit.

Ever Between the Light and Dark

Like the pendulum of a clock,
we swing back and forth,
ebbing and flowing
between the light and dark.
The dark is consuming;
to dwell in it is to sacrifice humanity;
in it lies death.
What they don't tell you
about death is that he has
such a seductive smile.
Looking into his grinning visage,
everything seems permissible,
nothing is forbidden
and the world seems to be made
just for you.
Then, shifting back into the light,
only then are the horrors of your deeds
laid bare before the looking light:
Life itself.
Life teaches us not to hate,
not to hurt. His smile assures us,
a warm embrace, insuring us of our safety.
But like blinders,
the problem with Life is that he is too limiting.
For his light and smile,
we cannot see the wolves sneaking up on us.
Life teaches us not to hate,
but Life itself hates Death.

The Devil's Coming to Town

I can hear him coming because
we've driven off God's light.
The devil's coming to town.

The barren church grounds
belies a tenebrous blight.
I can hear him coming now.

We exsanguinated our wound
not knowing it would wrong the right.
The devil's coming too. Towns

abandoned by The Profound
are embraced by the emperor of night.
I can hear him coming. Now

we despair at his unholy crown.
Like Icarus, we failed our flight.
The devil's coming to town.

As the unholy trumpets sound
and we fall, crippled with fright,
I can hear him coming now.
The devil's coming to town.

Nightmare Manifested

Horrors are brought low
to terrestrial realms,
where darkness bleeds into the corners of the room.
I am paralyzed, the demon of my nightmares
manifested to material evil.
The stretched skin that covers my walls
has begun to rot,
the fetid putrescence fills my nostrils,
and my thoughts are consumed by shadows and sinister machinations.
Ribbons of flesh lay as garland around my neck
perfuming the empty spaced with the stench of rot.
Putrefaction slicks the floors with liquid gore
and the acid rain created puddles of molten flesh.
All this fear is punctuated by an alarm.
I awake to find the corners vacant,
the shadows ebbed to a crawl.
Yet, I fear the union between foot and floor,
for under the bed, darkness still reigns supreme.

Coupon

Valid only in the U.S.,
Puerto Rico, and the
Virgin Islands,
because you aren't
worth a discount
elsewhere.
You're awfully smug
for a coupon lying
discarded at the
self-checkout,
Where I stood for
seven hours, for a
total of $56.
No, Nutella, I can't
afford you, for you
can't afford me,
not even a wide enough
space to write proper
stanzas.

Lost Fires

There it stood:
a bastion of hope
in the void of despair
Its flames licked up,
tasting the oxygen,
fighting for survival
in amidst a great swath
of black viscera that
seemed to sprout Tenebrae
to grab those who made a
break for the fire.
Could the fire withstand so
that someday it could heat
a lost soul? Can a fire
without fuel survive the
long night?

Reflection

Staring into the lake,
I saw it.
Full of bitterness and spite,
it glared back—
its smirk as a declaration,
an accusation of all missteps.
The eyes were the most detestable:
two lacerating points bleeding me
of all hope and joy,
reminding me of familiar sights.
Do I leap in after it or sail away?

Sorrow Sings Softly

Sorrow sings softly and sweet,
a lullaby that lulls a soul to sleep.
Its hooks sink in, a crawl—
injecting its venom, sticky and sweet,
into the heart,
a honey the oozes its way,
hardening in the chambers,
blinding our minds to the dangers.

Chapter V: Glimpses of Hope

Preface

In the preface to Chapter IV, I mentioned that I do not now view life with as much of a dour disposition as I used to. The poems in the following section are evidence of this shift in perspective. If you have read my previous book *Home Is Heavenward*, I wrote about a change in my spiritual life that has altered the way I live permanently for the better.

A great many of the poems in the following chapter focus on nostalgia, God, philosophy, and fulfillment. Some of these poems were written experimentally. For instance, the poem "A Message Written on Styrofoam Plates" was literally written on a Styrofoam plate. "Why?" one may ask. A young-adult Christ-centered ministry I helped run called Nomad used to have a worship night every month. We wanted these worship nights to be different so we would encourage worshipping in whatever manner you wanted to worship God. Me being a writer decided to write poetry. Wouldn't you know it though, I forgot my notebook at home. Necessity is the mother of invention so I scoured our church's kitchen for something I could write on. As it turned out, Styrofoam plates would be that medium. God uses the unexpected to create greatness.

While dividing my poems into categories, I had a hard time sorting a few poems. Much as the title of this book implies, I am forever a pendulum swinging back and forth between the light and dark. As such, some poems may not fit perfectly into either the dark or light categories and may be a shade of gray. For instance, "Nervous Habits" is largely negative but I feel as if the nervous habits I use as a coping mechanism make me feel less anxious, thus being a net positive.

As a whole, many of these poems are more recently written than previous ones, though not uniformly true. Many of my favorite poems are in this section and I hope you are able to glean as much insight and inspiration from them as I did when I wrote them.

Don-Don's Barn

We used to go down to Don-Don's barn
play in the muck till we were filthy
and dig a big hole around his pond and let it fill with water.
It looked like Yoo-hoo as it trickled in
spilling between the passage we'd dug for it.
Fill it up, like a hot tub, bathe in mud
like people paid thousands to fix themselves because they weren't
happy.
But we were just kids in the filth of animals. Happy.
We'd jump when we saw a crawdad float in
Think it was a lobster
But to us, it was a monster.
We'd go to the fire pit and poke long metal poles in,
put in feed sacks of synthetic fibers
that'd melt and look like marshmallow fluff on the end.
Then the poles'd get hot, sometimes burn our hands.
We'd let'm get red hot and run 'em over to the pond and douse them.
How the water'd boil and spit at being upset.
But we were delighted.
The emus in the fence next to us'd make that noise—
a noise that only emus make.
It's like a humming from the gut that radiates out.
You'd have to hear it to know what I'm talkin' about.
Down by the creek behind the pond,
there was a stump next to a little waterfall.
We'd hunt for frogs under it.
Some nights we would catch like 10 frogs.
Back then we didn't know a frog from a toad.
I still can't tell the difference.
They'd pee in our hands and make
that funny thrumming with their throats,
going in-and-out over and over again, trying to look inconspicuous.
As if they could just act cool
maybe we wouldn't notice we'd picked them up.

I'd always get scared when the Zebu came out.
He wasn't mean but a big bull is always to be feared by a kid.
We'd navigate to the other side of the barn.
Gramps would be feeding the cats and we'd watch him.
Descending out of nowhere, they came swarming to get a taste
of whatever was in those cans of stuff he gave them.
Inside the barns were bales of hay
and we'd put our shovels in there that
we used to dig the holes
we ran from when the lobsters came to get us.
Inside the feed shed, there were hedgehogs.
I can't remember their names now.
Probably something unoriginal like Spiney or Spike,
but as kids, you don't think about naming conventions
with as much scrutiny as adults.
They would make funny little oinking sounds
as they got their meals under heat lamps.
If we were lucky some nights Don-Don'd fire up the tractor.
When we were too big to sit on his lap,
he'd put on the basket attachment to the back.
It was a cage that had some padding inside to prevent us from gettin' cut.
He'd drive us around up and down hills on a hayride.
We'd shoot our fake guns at Graboids coming at us from underground.
We'd get banged up pretty bad,
but we'd come home covered in mud. Happy.
Shower off in the basement, cornbread, butter noodles, green beans, and fri-chik.
That's a night that'd get us into dreams in a hurry.

Still Higher

Lofted high, rescued from the pits of despair.
This rich air, it's mine as I fly high on prayer.
Internally, what was hardened has become infirmity.
Now I'll never die for Christ is mine, I shall not fry infernally.

Love is the current pushing passive to active.
Actions, like klaxons, quack massive attractions.
Beck and call, I can have it all, even though I fall,
I've lost nothing because loving has not made me stall.

Lord of all.
King of Kings
Higher than aspiration.
I sing your praises manifest.
Bless my life as you always have.
When I set your gifts aflame,
refine them to diamonds.
When I scald a note,
you turn death to melody.
Were grace to be felled by melody,
I sure would reside in Desiccation.
In the stead, I am alive in Elation.
Oh King of Kings.
Lord of all.
We of law delight in the freedom therein.
Wind is your breath.

Revivify

Eternal life, a light that cares.
A support whose love lifts above and bears.
Freedom given freely, a feeling never leaving,
I look to the sky, He died, came back alive, the Spirit breathing.

A flaming pyre of the living fire,
Burning the bondage of snare in mires.
A flare of compassion, panging, sustaining.
What I thought I lost I was really gaining.

A season in nature and season in Spirit,
in the leaves I see change, in the wind I hear it.

He is alive.

Home Is Here

I never used to have a home,
down dust lanes I passed.
I've seen rain run through cracked cement,
searching down to look for rest.
Leaves have blown in search of home.
They know that it is gone.
There is nothing for them here
but to be trod to dust
and meet the rainwater on its downward search.
I've seen curtains part and whispers uttered.
Their houses are not homes.   E
I have no house, but I have a home.   M
You see, the rainwater looks down in search of rest,   O
but what they seek is up.   H
I found it.
They will too.   K
After all, as ashes turn to ashes   C
and dust to dust   A
soon the water will ascend back into the heavens   B

Passage of Time

That which was, and is, and is still to come
must command time.
To command one must be over.
To be over, one must be higher.
Therefore, if one was, and is, and is still to come,
He must be above time and command it.
Time, as we have known it, is a force,
pre-existent of human thought.
That which commands time must also be
pre-existent.

The Fantastic Pots and Pans of Mr. Marvelous

Step right up and try Mr. Marvelous' cure-all tonic! You can't disagree with the results!
-Mr. Marvelous, Snake Oil Extraordinaire

Our covered wagon stumbles
to forests old, to the next wellspring of life.
Among the frocks,
among the sacks,
clang us pans and pots.

Mr. Pot sits in rusty hue,
still serving his purpose,
heating and cooking with the best of them.
His life's been long.
The dings and scrapes are his proof.
He tried to warn me
of this line of work saying
"Get out now!"
but he's probably just telling
one of his war stories again.

Then there's Ms. Pan.
No, not Mrs. Pan, Ms. Pan.
Shhh…be quiet…
God only knows what she'll stir up if she wakes.
She's liable to spit oil, burn the food,
maybe heat the wrong way and produce
something that isn't quite edible.
Come now, don't make fun of her.
It isn't her fault that Mr. Marvelous
always chooses her sister.

And of course, there's Mr. Vat…
You couldn't miss him.
That overblown, obtuse, cocky son-of-a-bitch is always bragging about his size.
I get it. He's big. Too bad
it takes him so long to heat up
that the rest of us are done and in the bed before he even wakes up.
I heard he's the reason that Ms. Pan is the way she is.

We can't forget Skillet,
though, to be frank,
he is quite forgettable.
All you need to know is that he's big
and about as deep as a nail pairing.

Then there's good ole Tea Kettle—
more often used for coffee than tea.
He doesn't care for the taste
but he's just happy to help out.
His whistle always sings a song of the best virtues of life.
If you're looking for a bit of cheer
on days where there's none to be found,
he is always willing to have a chat.

Lastly, there's Broken Pot—the one with the bullet hole.
He can't cook worth a damn anymore, but I respect him.
He saved Mr. Marvelous from angry customers last year.
Those were the ones who begged to differ with the results.
I saw Mr. Marvelous thinking about throwing him out
but he couldn't bring himself to do it.
If it wasn't for him, I'd be used in some filthy saloon.

Welcome to our job
alongside the Pacific Railroad,
tracing towns and camps.
Our clanks and pops sing a melody
of harmony between man, machine
and the trees which drink from the nearby river.

A Message Written on Styrofoam Plates

A vessel desolate,
Above soil I rise,
called by compulsion,
my stone
erodes to heart, revealing life within.
The stones speak with commandment,
etching law with my fabric.
I taste my new self—the sweetness
serene mornings trilling with birdsong.
Just as stones remain for eons,
this NEW testifies to its eternity.
The granite is testament to eyes,
called to vision by that which dwarfs eternity.
When nothing is to now and now is to past,
He who dates the stones remains in past.
                                        Now.
                                                Future.
Trees are but saplings, pebbles
but mountains, and we are as the thought
of yesterday—
gone before blossom.
Mountain melodies are carried
                              on the wind for an age
but an idea outlives
the most virile of ancients.
Yet even these are but seconds
to a century.
I was born a slave to time,
but my chains of slavery were
        shattered
by He who stands
as mediator between
term's end and infinite
                                                suspension.

There could never be a
doubt of the power
of an idea persisting outside of life.
This idea is God.
God is my God.

Secret Garden

There was a place
back when I was a kid,
where time worked at cross-purposes to industry.
Downtown Newton had its share of wonders.
There was that cannon
someone had left loaded unknowingly,
Which created what is now
a memorialized hole in a flower shop.
There was the historic museum
where the juniors took us seniors,
abducted from school
to figure out the theme for prom—
my friend and I broke the handcuffs they put on us.
The most special place though, was the garden.
After lunch at Callahan's Café—
the owner Roy always gave me a Krackle—
my dad and I would cross the street to visit the Secret Garden.
The garden was simple.
A small winding path parted
a yard filled with burning vibrancy.
Bleeding roses and burning carnations
lit the world
of concrete aflame with life:
a gardener's soul siphoned.
Hedge walls secluded this Eden—hidden—Prajña.
This was *my* garden.
Others visited it, but *I* knew it.
I want to return,
but I fear what might've become of it.
For every tree, there is an axe.
Perhaps it would be better to leave it be.
For now it might be another boy's garden,
but in that singular point in time,
it was mine.

Little Wheaten Kisses

The smell of warm puppy breath—
not wholly pleasant, but at the same time,
comforting, homey, with touches of sulfur.
The look of trust in their eyes:
"Hold me daddy. Don't let me go."
Black noses that they quite haven't grown into,
look like overstuffed olives—
slightly salty and moist.
Their golden fur glistens in the sunlight—
the pot of gold at the end of the rainbow.
It is soft, far softer than any earthly material,
yes, this is certainly something divine.
Both of their ears rise and fall with their moods,
going from overjoyed to scared to sleepy all within
the amount of time it takes to boil water.
I am sleeping. Their cold noses touch me.
"Take us out, daddy."
Little caricatures of bears,
their gonks, grawrls, and gurrrrs
are musical melodies
melting magically into my ears.
Their feet, sometimes toasty,
sometimes a bit cold,
stick out as pillows for their heads.
Their eyes are slits as they sleep,
twitching nervously at whatever dogs dream about.
Trying at times? Oh yes, certainly.
They've driven me mad. Wheaten madness.
Every ounce of anger is worth it
for those little wheaten kisses.

April 4, 1968

I saw the branch peeking through the hole in the fence,
a newborn baby surveying the world.
The branch swayed in the morning breeze,
tasting his freedom
that his mother
had only seen from the cage.
But that little branch, as only little branches can do,
fought and struggled, boring a hole through its cage
till the plastic and metal
gave way to the sweet taste
of the blissful alternative.

The hole's radius peeled outward like a bullet wound.
It would only be a matter of time
till some overzealous gardener or
vindictive upright one
would come along
breaking the branch,
snapping it off before it got to grow,
ripping it from its mother's grasp.
But the branch didn't care.
He knew his life would be much better here,
dancing in the wind, free at last.

Nervous Habits

I trace my knuckles
choosing the best
knowing the satisfaction
comes from errors in my brain's software.
I rock the knuckle
till my fingers numb
and knuckles blush.

I sink my teeth
into my bottom lip,
repeating now, and later,
knowing this satisfaction
sparks from a loose wire in my circuitry.
I chew until my lips blister
and pain ceases my prostration.

I cross the skin between my fingers,
webbing stretching
then retracting
knowing the satisfaction
ekes from a rusted cog in my machine.
I cross until I callous,
unable to bear the feeling of my own hands.

I scrunch my top lip,
to peak then valley,
feeling the whiskers scrape,
ticking my lip
knowing the satisfaction
comes from laughs and anxiety
that I can't quite place.
I fold my lip
until the world seems right again.

Live Now

Live now
for the times is right.
The mountains stretch,
armies of fire, birch, and oak,
all triumphant.
The rivers flow free,
coursing down;
away from fear,
away from worry,
their problems flung far
over the edge of the earth.
Creations sings the song
of the Great Creator.
They, an echo of His resplendence,
glory, and might.
Time has no sway.
Forces of evil cower,
fearing the strength of the whale roads lining the seas.
How then can evil crush life
if they fear the paths on which it treads?
Sing softly of the setting sun,
for triumphant Dawn always rises.

In Defence of the Lamp

During the blackest of nights
when the moon's light is only
a nail paring of what it
once was and there's work to do,
it recuses me of my
most pressing predicaments.
It's long silver fingers reach
ever upward to grab the
head, forever pulling on
its visor to contain its
full glory lest I become
blind and unable to work.
The small scratch on the base tells
of long nights of projects and
far too much coffee, letting
its gaze guide me onward to
another complete paper.
And not once has it complained.
No batting of its single
eye to inform me that it
is time to go to bed.
It just stands, singing its song,
one of the sun and flashlights,
when the world isn't obscured.
So, on the nights like tonight,
I dare not protest too much
for I could be in darkness
instead of bathing in its
calming, resplendent glory
that guides me throughout my work.

Flying

Gravity is subverted,
As I go into the cosmos—infinity.
Aloft in the ether, I'll never fall in my ascent to divinity
With his legs straight and tall.
The monuments of man—so minuscule—like ants
under my gaze. Above all
Fear, worry, and doubt in a place where
I'm free to shout, and all things are cast in a new light.
As I hold my Father's hand with my own
Small boy's hands,
Entwined in flight,
He treats it as an honor.

Running Ever Toward the Sun

Toward the horizon,
toward the setting sun.
To just catch a glimpse
of the power within...
its full shine would surely be too much
for me to handle.
I would be overwhelmed.
I would be blinded
by the sheer magnificent
glory contained within.

This quest to just touch it...
it is like Ahab's quest for his whale.
Will my fate be likened to his?
I hope that one day
I will be able to reach it.
I fear that my power
could not even come close
to being a parody of that of the sun's.
If only I had known then that
if I had waited,
the sun would've come to me.

Shine On

Like a flame in the night,
burning ever bright, guiding man
and beast alike, you shine
as gold amongst the mire.
Beneath the setting sun, as the ice
creeps ever closer, you are the shield
which splits the firmament.
The wicked will come to dig in their fingers,
to snare their unearned treasure.
But your bright light, sending the night alight,
guides the wayfarer home.
For a time will come
when all lights dim
and not a soul can be found.
For times most dim and times most dark,
shine on forevermore.

The Stargazer

I look up into
the sky at night and
see infinity.
Thousands of eyes staring
back at me
giving me hope
and affirmation of my own
existence.
If I am being observed
then I must be real
and that fills me
with joy.

Warum

Crawling, I peeked over
seeing the great expanse.
How could such an ocean
of memories and meaning
be full of such palpable
nothingness?
Is this a great expanse
or the tip of a pen?
Perhaps the face of the divine
is peeking just below the surface
or perhaps it is beaming from the depths.

Half

I am an empty vessel
into which a spirit
must be poured.
As branches cannot
support themselves
without a trunk,
I cannot live without
a spirit.
Some people choose to fill
the chasm with the vices
of the world.
These things provide temporary
pleasure.
Only the Spirit gives
everlasting joy.

The Super-Pets

When I was little
I called my stuffed animals
The Super-Pets.
They were the center
of the toy collective
that was
my childhood.
My parents told me that
one day
I would stop playing with The Super-Pets
when I got older.
I would meet friends.
I would fall in love.
I would get a job.
I would go to college.
I was horrified.
Surely this inseparable love
would never be
severed.
I vowed that I
would never stop
playing with The Super Pets.
But parents are visionaries for children.
I grew older while The Super-Pets
stayed the same—
trapped in that moment from childhood
where the inanimate becomes
gyrations, rotation, dance, and song—
when a set of plastic foods becomes
a restaurant—
when a soft, cool blanket offers comfort
in the hot nights of adolescence—
where sitting and listening to Hank the Cowdog
and sorting Neopets trading cards

is the best way to spend an evening.
Those days are past me.
I don't play with The Super Pets anymore.
Most have gone on to other families
or destroyed during the dark years
of growing up;
It seems we always destroy what we love.
However, in my closet,
a small contingent remains.
They wait in silence
staring through the muddled plastic,
hoping that one day their friend will return.
And I do, from time to time,
as we return to our childhood friends.
But the magic is lost.
We have but a momentary encounter
to exchange pleasantries,
but go on our way,
the connection severed.
But we never let go.
I will never play with The Super-Pets again.
They will stay with me though.
In my plastic box.
In my memory.
In my heart.

About the Author

Alexander Lowe is a writer hailing from Hickory, North Carolina. He graduated from Catawba Valley Community College with an Associates in Art and from Appalachian State University with a Bachelor of Arts in English with a concentration in Creative Writing. He is currently working on a degree in Engineering Technologies. He released his first book *The Spirit of Joy* in 2018. He released his second book *Home Is Heavenward* in 2020.

He is a practicing Christian and attends church at IChurch in Hickory, North Carolina. He came to truly know the Lord during his Senior year of college. He served as an administrator for a young-adult ministry called Nomad for two years. He edited the English translation of Pastor Clary Rodriguez's book *Under the Power of Who You Are* in 2021. He currently is edited two books for Dr. Tom Jackson, a chaplain living in Fletcher, North Carolina.

He enjoys relaxing, playing video games, and loving on his four dogs.

Made in the USA
Monee, IL
18 September 2021

77440238R00079